Semper Creo

365 Days of Creative Discipline

Creativity is a skill and is built through consistency.

The goal of any skill is improvement. Creativity is no different. No one is "born creative". Some make a more conscious effort to see the world in unique ways and express it. Out of the box thinking spurs the production of everything around us from workout habits and finding cures to disease, to building skylines and designing new inventions for human progress.
Creativity begins with practice. Sketching prompts inspire thought. Sketching daily builds the habit of thinking creatively. Sometimes, the quality of your sketch will satisfy you. Many times it won't. The skill you are focusing on isn't drawing; it's thinking in ways you haven't thought before.

When you build the habit of sketching, you'll be surprised by how your thinking changes. First, your drawing skill *will* improve through effort and habit. Second, your creativity will become a tool you can use in every area of your life. The problems you face will have new solutions inspired by your new habit of mind. Your world will become more vibrant with opportunity. You can look at the world and be immediately entertained by the mundane, the simple and the otherwise dull.

Your mind is a wonderful machine and creativity is its superpower!

How to use this sketchbook :

Spontaneity is critical. Do not preview prompts. I recommend starting from the first prompt and working forward, but you can use the prompts in any order.

- Set a timer for 10 minutes.
- Flip to the page and read the prompt.
- Sketch your interpretation of the prompt.
- Read one prompt and complete one sketch daily.

You can play music, pull up a reference photo (not all of us know what a heron looks like!), and use any drawing tool you please. The goal is to build the habit of thinking creatively and interpreting those thoughts through sketch.

Inktober Bonus!

During the month of October it is a tradition among many creatives to jot out one ink sketch per day. Usually, the themes will follow the Halloween season.
You can find Inktober prompts from pages 274 to 304.

Good luck and have fun!

Semper Creo…Always Create

1. Sketch a tiny circus on your head

2. Sketch something that moves fast

3. Sketch an alien insect

4. Sketch your brain in "Panic Mode"

5. Sketch what you ate today if it became alive

6. Sketch a monster

7. Sketch the best roller coaster ever

8. Sketch a villain

9. Sketch a giant

10.   Sketch a one man band

11.   Sketch a scene from your favorite book

12.   Sketch a subterranean world

13.   Sketch a western outlaw

14.   Sketch a shark with a bellyache

15. Sketch an astronaut having a bad day

16.   Sketch a door to another universe

17.   Sketch a place where you feel at peace

18.   Sketch a spider who wants to be friends

19.   Sketch something metal

20. Sketch a character from a children's book

21. Sketch an invasion from space

22.   Sketch a snake with hands

23. Sketch a kangaroo with an attitude problem

24.   Sketch a mean machine

25. Sketch the feeling of being alone

26.   Sketch a ballet

27.   Sketch a pretty little flower

28.   Sketch a small metropolis

29.   Sketch a monkey delivering the mail

30. Sketch 'Nowhere'

31. Sketch an entire battle

32.   Sketch something you've learned from an elder/mentor

33. Sketch something wonderful

34. Sketch an iconic duo

35. Sketch what you're feeling right now

36.   Sketch a place you want to go

37. Sketch something that fills you with joy

38. Sketch a cherished memory

39.   Sketch something loopy, crazy, bizzare and wacky

40.   Sketch your favorite food

41. Sketch something nostalgic for you

42.   Sketch something sweet

43.   Sketch something slow

44.   Sketch a lazy good time

45.   Sketch something epic

46.   Sketch an action scene

47.   Sketch a turkey on the run

48.   Sketch a snow animal

49.   Sketch something you love about winter

50.   Sketch something worth waiting for

51.   Sketch something cold

52.   Sketch an interesting looking snowman

53.   Sketch something cozy

54. Sketch something your parents like

55.   Sketch something mischievous

56.   Sketch a cool pair of glasses that you would wear

57. Sketch something elegant

58.   Sketch an irritated owl

59.   Sketch something intimidating

60.   Sketch a fighter

61. Sketch an ant/alligator hybrid

62. Sketch a leviathan

63. Sketch a song you like as an image

64.   Sketch something relaxing

65.   Sketch a weapon that makes everything funny

66. Sketch a no good terrible very bad day

67. Sketch a tortoise boxing a rabbit

68. Sketch a spider on his first day of high school

69.   Sketch a workout routine for a worm

70.   Sketch a space cowboy

71. Sketch the last thing that made you laugh

72.   Sketch a bird in love

73.   Sketch where the road ends

74. Sketch something that reminds you of Friday

75.   Sketch "Love"

76.   Sketch a cold, cold day

77.   Sketch a moment of change

78. Sketch something lost

79. Sketch "infinity"

80. Sketch the blues

81.   Sketch a happy reunion

82.   Sketch "Discipline"

83. Sketch what you want to be remembered for

84.   Sketch some magic

85.   Sketch something across the world

86.   Sketch a fight between two dragons

87. Sketch "Time"

88.   Sketch a dinosaur in the city

89. Sketch a diesel truck drinking coffee

90.   Sketch an island of misfit toys

91.   Sketch something flying

92.   Sketch yourself when you're bored

93. Sketch something ridiculous

94.   Sketch your brain in "Creativity" mode

95.   Sketch something painful

96.   Sketch a scene of pandemonium

97. Sketch a little miracle

98.   Sketch an elaborate trap

99.   Sketch something you're tired of

100. Sketch an animal that freaks you out

101. Sketch a duel between mules

102. Sketch a messy room

103. Sketch a life in a single sketch

104. Sketch a happy thought

105. Sketch a long journey

106. Sketch a walking tree

107. Sketch an ocean in space

108. Sketch a fruit working out

109. Sketch a police officer rooster

110. Sketch a mouse's house

111. Sketch a hungry robot

112. Sketch a building designed by a clown

113. Sketch a funny nose

114. Sketch something deep in the ocean

115. Sketch a lizard/spider hybrid

116. Sketch a dancing shadow

117. Sketch something heroic

118. Sketch a crocodile on vacation

119. Sketch something you do on a rainy day

120. Sketching something wild

121. Sketch a T-Rex chilling in the pool

122. Sketch living lightning

123. Sketch an army of butterflies

124. Sketch traffic for spaceships

125. Sketch a megalodon

126. Sketch a terrible advertisement

127. Sketch a mud monster

128. Sketch something out of style

129. Sketch the furthest corner of space

130. Sketch something bittersweet

131. Sketch a hairstyle you'd never get

132. Sketch something durable

133. Sketch something cool

134. Sketch a wasteland

135. Sketch a lizard king

136. Sketch a bug having an x-ray

137. Sketch something old

138. Sketch "Wisdom"

139. Sketch a bat in a hat looking for his cat

140. Sketch 'Xylophobia' (fear of wooded areas)

141. Sketch something that makes you think of home

142. Sketch a fish city

143. Sketch a space alien zoo

144. Sketch a raging bull

145. Sketch something you worked hard for

146. Sketch one trait of a good father

147. Sketch one trait of a good mother

148. Sketch something special only to you

149. Sketch an iron pig

150. Sketch a difficult choice

151. Sketch 'Mercy'

152. Sketch something extraordinary

153. Sketch a runaway cheese

154. Sketch a dinosaur on a swing set

155. Sketch somes ants wearing pants as they water their plants

156. Sketch a parakeet as a plumber

157. Sketch an underwater party

158. Sketch a mean gang of pigeons

159. Sketch something beautiful to you

160. Sketch something small

161. Sketch a bear washing his car

162. Sketch a choir of toucans

163. Sketch a muffin welding on an oil rig

164. Sketch a healthy choice

165. Sketch a mushroom rock band

166. Sketch a war of the worlds

167. Sketch 'Waiting'

168. Sketch a dream a gorilla might have

169. Sketch a trailer park golf course

170. Sketch two octopi dancing together

171. Sketch a heartbroken snail

172. Sketch a new chapter of life

173. Sketch two airplanes on a date

174. Sketch a happy bug in love

175. Sketch a cactus sitting in church

176. Sketch a funny cheeseburger

177. Sketch a lonely potato

178. Sketch a steamroller trying to tiptoe

179. Sketch something quiet

180. Sketch an eskimo at a pool party

181. Sketch where the wild things are

182. Sketch a duck stuck in the muck

183. Sketch a jungle scene

184. Sketch a betta fish in a jazz band

185. Sketch a growing storm

186. Sketch a paranoid pine tree

187. Sketch a fox in a new pair of socks

188. Sketch a moment under the stars

189. Sketch an imaginary way that jelly is made

190. Sketch the last item you lost

191. Sketch/design your own skyscraper

192. Sketch a squirrel playing guitar

193. Sketch a scary gym teacher

194. Sketch a toilet with legs

195. Sketch something Egyptian

196. Sketch a police dog

197. Sketch a great moment in history

198. Sketch a map

199. Sketch a sunrise on another planet

200. Sketch a hamster as the President of the United States

201. Sketch a sad goodbye

202. Sketch a mouse battling a lion

203. Sketch a fun time for a rocking chair

204. Sketch 'Hope'

205. Sketch what a bug might be thinking

206. Sketch a stroke of good fortune

207. Sketch a royal ball

208. Sketch a tornado riding a horse

209. Sketch a bar of chocolate suntanning

210. Sketch a party of alpacas

211. Sketch an electric koala

212. Sketch bigfoot

213. Sketch a pair of pants driving a muscle car

214. Sketch something dangerous

215. Sketch two opposites

216. Sketch a heron with a headache

217. Sketch a walrus teaching literature class

218. Sketch a teddy bear with the blues

219. Sketch a rich catfish

220. Sketch a calm Autumn morning

221. Sketch a snake with a cold

222. Sketch a high speed chase

223. Sketch a mountain resort

224. Sketch the world's strongest grain of rice

225. Sketch the inside of a house with no gravity

226. Sketch an orange running a marathon

227. Sketch your fingers having an argument

228. Sketch a fairy drinking dairy

229. Sketch a dog celebrating Fourth of July

230. Sketch a lug nut shooting a longbow

231. Sketch a computer surviving in the jungle

232. Sketch 'Anger'

233. Sketch a cool pair of wings

234. Sketch the biggest feet on the smallest person

235. Sketch a lampshade as a lawyer

236. Sketch a wildfire

237. Sketch a frog playing the banjo

238. Sketch a tooth named Ruth

239. Sketch a chain made out of rain

240. Sketch your favorite song

241. Sketch some house cats having a bake sale

242. Sketch a giraffe as a garbage man

243. Sketch a rodeo clown in an office building

244. Sketch a hole in the sky

245. Sketch a bacteria

246. Sketch a snake stuck in a knot

247. Sketch a kid's ultimate sandcastle

248. Sketch lightbulbs having a family reunion

249. Sketch a dangerous rabbit

250. Sketch a cowboy riding a bumper car

251. Sketch a stress free moment

252. Sketch a family of pigs on a road trip

253. Sketch Pinocchio as a politician

254. Sketch a dangerous voyage

255. Sketch a sunrise without using any lines

256. Sketch a bee on an underwater excursion

257. Sketch a new kind of instrument

258. Sketch a paint brush playing catch with a pencil

259. Sketch Godzilla waiting in line at the Post Office

260. Sketch a skunk in prison

261. Sketch 'Silence'

262. Sketch something that made you smile today

263. Sketch a book in a good mood

264. Sketch a wizard trapped in an ice cube

265. Sketch a giant bunny vs. the U.S. military

266. Sketch a crawfish sneaking into a movie theater

267. Sketch a piece of toast riding rotisserie chicken

268. Sketch a bull baking cookies

269. Sketch a turkey taking a tiger's tea

270. Sketch a lemon going roller skating

271. Sketch an angry potato

272. Sketch a brave explorer

273. Sketch a haunted hound dog

274. Sketch a banana as a jack-o-lantern

275. Sketch a granny vampire's dentures

276. Sketch a ghost at the barber

277. Sketch the grim reaper grabbing groceries

278. Sketch Dracula's kitchen

279. Sketch The Boogeyman

280. Sketch a nightmare

281. Sketch a ghost ship

282. Sketch a werewolf having a cup of tea

283. Sketch a ghoul on his way to school

284. Sketch a mummy and her mommy

285. Sketch a zombie zebra

286. Sketch a smoking scarecrow

287. Sketch a monster on his day off of work

288. Sketch a spider going Trick or Treating

289. Sketch a beast in a belltower

290. Sketch a skeleton mouse in a haunted house

291. Sketch a pirate carving pumpkins

292. Sketch a voodoo vulture casting spells

293. Sketch Mr. and Mrs. Frankenstein on a date

294. Sketch a Halloween parade

295. Sketch a haunted circus

296. Sketch a living shadow

297. Sketch a bone xylophone

298. Sketch an escape from the grave

299. Sketch a zombie in math class

300. Sketch a hillbilly vampire

301. Sketch what lurks in the dark

302. Sketch a ghoul in the pool looking really cool

303. Sketch Acrophobia (Fear of Heights)

304. Sketch a city of jack-o-lanterns

305. Sketch your primary emotion

306. Sketch something that gets on your nerves

307. Sketch your brain when you're daydreaming

308. Sketch a T-Rex trying to zip up his jacket

309. Sketch Santa going through the drive thru

310. Sketch a maze and then complete the maze

311. Sketch a staring contest

312. Sketch 'Doubt'

313. Sketch a balloon in a saloon

314. Sketch an outlaw ostrich

315. Sketch a change of heart

316. Sketch something you miss

317. Sketch a lonely drive

318. Sketch a stress monster

319. Sketch "Warmth"

320. Sketch "Brain Fog"

321. Sketch a monkey using a lawnmower

322. Sketch an unlucky shamrock

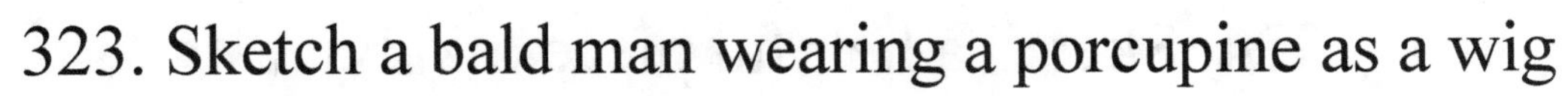

323. Sketch a bald man wearing a porcupine as a wig

324. Sketch a helpful piece of advice

325. Sketch a whale in a wedding veil

326. Sketch an imaginary friend

327. Sketch a sad story in one image

328. Sketch a memory you hope you never lose

329. Sketch a martian

330. Sketch "Chaos"

331. Sketch your train of thought

332. Sketch something delicate

333. Sketch a baby duck playing football

334. Sketch an anaconda with arachnophobia (fear of arachnids)

335. Sketch a giant snowball fight

336. Sketch a winter fireside

337. Sketch a candy factory

338. Sketch a rabbit drinking espresso

339. Sketch a gift you received

340. Sketch Santa's GPS

341. Sketch an image of "Reborn"

342. Sketch a cookie sunning in the oven

343. Sketch turtle jumping hurdles

344. Sketch a sailboat in space

345. Sketch a daddy long leg spider roller skating

346. Sketch gremlin hiding in a stocking

347. Sketch a Christmas village

348. Sketch an octopus toy maker

349. Sketch a home in the hollow of a tree

350. Sketch a eskimo rodeo

351. Sketch bar scene of Christmas elves

352. Sketch an explosion of color (without using color)

353. Sketch a made up character named Wombat Rickles

354. Sketch gym rat

355. Sketch the anatomy of a cartoon clown

356. Sketch something you're looking forward to

357. Sketch "Excitement"

358. Sketch a snowflake, a flame and pebble playing poker

359. Sketch a house at the bottom of the ocean

360. Sketch a sneeze

361. Sketch an image with something hidden in it

362. Sketch "Nervousness"

363. Sketch an unfortunate superpower

364. Sketch a shampoo bottle with a surprising message on the label

365. Sketch "The End"

www.ingramcontent.com/pod-product-compliance
Lightning Source LLC
Chambersburg PA
CBHW081924120726
47997CB00010B/3024